Land Use

Valerie Weber and Janice Redlin

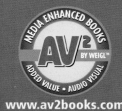

MEDIA ENHANCED BOOKS

AV2 BY WEIGL

ADDED VALUE · AUDIO VISUAL

www.av2books.com

AV² provides enriched content that supplements and complements this book. Weigl's AV² books strive to create inspired learning and engage young minds in a total learning experience.

Your AV² Media Enhanced books come alive with...

Go to www.av2books.com, and enter this book's unique code.

Audio
Listen to sections of the book read aloud.

Key Words
Study vocabulary, and complete a matching word activity.

BOOK CODE

R926791

Video
Watch informative video clips.

Quizzes
Test your knowledge.

AV² by Weigl brings you media enhanced books that support active learning.

Embedded Weblinks
Gain additional information for research.

Slide Show
View images and captions, and prepare a presentation.

Download the AV² catalog at www.av2books.com/catalog

Try This!
Complete activities and hands-on experiments.

... and much, much more!

AV² Online Navigation on page 48

Published by AV² by Weigl
350 5ᵗʰ Avenue, 59ᵗʰ Floor
New York, NY 10118

Website: www.av2books.com   www.weigl.com

Library of Congress Control Number: 2013941891
ISBN 978-1-62127-439-1 (hardcover)
ISBN 978-1-62127-445-2 (softcover)
ISBN 978-1-62127-835-1 (single-user eBook)
ISBN 978-1-48961-722-4 (multi-user eBook)

Printed in the United States of America in North Mankato, Minnesota
1 2 3 4 5 6 7 8 9 0 17 16 15 14 13

062013
WEP220513

Weigl acknowledges Getty Images as its primary image supplier for this title.

Every reasonable effort has been made to trace ownership and to obtain permission to reprint copyright material. The publishers would be pleased to have any errors or omissions brought to their attention so that they may be corrected in subsequent printings.

Project Coordinator: Aaron Carr
Art Director: Terry Paulhus

Land Use

CONTENTS

Introduction to Land Use

Much of life on Earth depends on the land and the soil that covers a large portion of it. For thousands of years, farmers have depended on the land and soil to produce crops. The forests, fields, and plains that sustain a variety of vegetation and animals all grow in soil. If that dirt is eroded, or washed away by winds and rain, plants cannot grow. If poisons pollute the land, plants die. Food becomes scarce. Without diverse plant life, animal species die out. People cannot survive.

Impact of Land Use

"Scientists estimate that half of the **topsoil** on the planet has been lost in the past 150 years. Poor farming methods are the main causes of soil erosion."

What Soil Is Made Of

"Soil is a complex material. It is made up of particles from rocks, **minerals**, water, and gases. It includes animal droppings and bits from dead plants and animals."

Land Use and Abuse

"Every year, more than 22 billion tons (20 billion tonnes) of soil are swept away by wind and **precipitation**. Storms take up soil loosened by poor farming and herding techniques."

Protecting the Soil

"Many governments around the world are encouraging the use of conservation agriculture (CA). Farms using CA do little or no **tilling**. Seeds are drilled directly into the soil."

Impact of Land Use

KEY CONCEPTS

1 Farming Methods and Erosion

2 Desertification and Deforestation

3 Loss of Biodiversity and Wildlife

4 Waterway Silt

5 Fertilizer and Animal Runoff

About 90 percent of the food eaten today comes from land-based agriculture. However, soil is being lost or **contaminated** on a vast scale. The causes of soil **degradation** are many. Soil is eroded or covered with water. Using channels or sprinklers, farmers bring water to their crops. These irrigation methods pull salts or acids to the land's surface, reducing its ability to support plant life. Constant farming with heavy machinery compacts the dirt, making it difficult for shoots to poke out of the soil. Forests are cut down, and grasslands are overgrazed. The roots of trees and grasses no longer hold the soil in place.

1 Farming Methods and Erosion

The world's population is more than 7 billion. Scientists estimate that number will increase to 8 billion by 2025. As the population increases, more and more land is cleared for growing crops, raising animals, housing, and businesses. The ability of Earth's soil to produce enough food for all these people is being stretched to the limit in some regions. Giant agricultural businesses are replacing small family farms. Their farming methods often damage the soil with chemicals or cause it to blow or wash away.

Scientists estimate that half of the topsoil on the planet has been lost in the past 150 years. Poor farming methods are the main causes of soil erosion. Often, farmers remove native plants that bind the soil through their root systems. Grasses, trees, and other plants also absorb some of the Sun's heat, preventing soil from

drying out. They protect the soil from the direct impact of heavy rainfall, as well. Remove the plant life, and the soil is easily whisked away by the first downpour or gust of wind.

Trees and other vegetation also act as windbreaks. They reduce the amount of soil that wind blows from the tops of fields. Wind erosion scatters the topsoil so that it is lost to agriculture.

Major Types and Causes of Soil Erosion

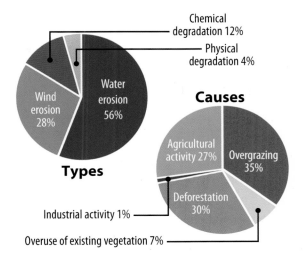

Chemical degradation 12%
Physical degradation 4%
Water erosion 56%
Wind erosion 28%
Types

Causes
Agricultural activity 27%
Overgrazing 35%
Deforestation 30%
Industrial activity 1%
Overuse of existing vegetation 7%

The third largest island on Earth, Borneo was once covered in rainforest. Logging companies and owners of plantations of oil palm trees have cut down much of world's oldest rainforest.

2 Desertification and Deforestation

Land abuse has been going on since the invention of agriculture. Some ancient civilizations had good soil that was ruined by overuse. Mesopotamia was an area of the Middle East located between the Tigris and Euphrates Rivers. Between about 10,000 and 5,000 BC, various civilizations lived in the area. However, the land was farmed until all soil **nutrients** that supported crops were gone.

Then and now, some farming problems include the overgrazing of land. Nothing can grow properly when herds of goats, sheep, or cows eat every new shoot. When all plant life on arid land is gone, the land becomes a desert. This process is called desertification.

Overgrazing in some countries is a result of population increase. In Africa, for example, more animals may be needed to feed growing families from the same area of land. Worldwide, overgrazing accounts for more than one-third of all soil degradation through erosion and desertification.

Deforestation is another cause of soil erosion. Deforestation is the cutting down of forests for lumber or to clear land for agriculture, construction, or other human activities. For example, since the mid-1970s, 17 percent of the Amazon rainforest has been cut down. This area is equal to the size of France. Scientists think that about 80 percent of the world's ancient forests have been destroyed. A large proportion of this loss has occurred within the past 50 years.

Should Grazing and Farming Be Controlled on Dry Lands Bordering the Sahara Desert?

Dry lands are arid and semiarid areas bordering deserts. The Sahel is a narrow area south of the Sahara Desert in Africa. It covers 270,000 square miles (700,000 square kilometers) and stretches from Senegal in the west to Sudan in the east. This region has been damaged by overfarming and overgrazing. Erosion is widespread.

It was not always this way. Nomadic herders once kept their animals on the move, so that no single area became overgrazed. The amount of agriculture in any area was limited by the amount of rain that fell.

United Nations Environment Programmme
We want to restore the Sahel's degraded ecosystem. We need people to plant trees that yield food. Grazing animals will eat the shoots from these trees.

Hausa
We are farmers in the Sahel. We need this land to raise crops, but we worry about the effects of overgrazing. Animals' hoofs compact the soil and kill the grass. Erosion results, and farming becomes impossible.

Fulani
For centuries, our people have been nomads and used the Sahel for grazing. If we need to roam the Sahel to feed our herds, we should be allowed to do so.

Governments of the Sahel Region
We owe money to international organizations. Grazing animals provide meat to eat. We should also raise cash crops that will feed many people and help repay our debt.

For	Supportive	Undecided	Unsupportive	Against

3 Loss of Biodiversity and Wildlife

Biodiversity refers to the variety of plants, animals, **fungi**, and germs living in various habitats. Over time, species have adapted to the conditions in particular habitats. If a habitat is damaged or destroyed, some types of living things may not be able to survive and will be lost forever. These species are valuable because other plants and animals depend on them. They may also be possible sources of medicine and food for people.

Turning over the land with a mechanical plow or handheld hoe is called tillage. Exposing soil to the elements, such as wind, sunlight, frost, and rain, can cause erosion and nutrient loss. This damages soil biodiversity, especially in large fields planted with only one crop. Earthworms and millions of other creatures help keep soil healthy and fertile. Plowing the topsoil disturbs soil ecosystems. The organisms die off.

When fertilizers are applied to cropland, plants take only what they need. The rest, which may be as much as half of the original amount, remains in the soil. It may also be lost through runoff, which is water or other liquids that drain freely off the land's surface.

Contaminated soil or runoff carries its chemicals into the sea, where they can damage plants and animals. For example, corals in areas along the Great Barrier Reef in Australia are dying. About 80 percent of the land near the Great Barrier Reef is farmland. Farmers use fertilizers that contain high amounts of phosphorous and **nitrates**. These chemicals run off into the ocean, where they promote the growth of **phytoplankton**. Crown-of-thorn starfish larvae thrive on this phytoplankton. They grow to be adults who eat corals. Scientists have also shown that coral reefs near agricultural lands have fewer kinds of corals and fish than reefs farther from farmland.

Excess fertilizer turns some areas of the oceans into dead zones, where most forms of sea life have died off.

4 Waterway Silt

After precipitation falls to Earth, it begins to move according to the laws of gravity. The ground absorbs some rainfall, but most of it flows downhill as runoff. The type of soil, the height and slant of the land, and the plants covering it all affect the amount of runoff. Runoff from cultivated land often carries excess soil that can reduce water quality.

"In the United States, the cost of damage from silt may exceed $10 billion a year."

Excess soil also clouds the water, reducing the amount of sunlight getting to **aquatic** plants. It reduces the ability of fish to see their prey. This makes it harder for fish to feed. In addition, silt can clog the delicate gills of fish, making it harder for them to breathe. Excess silt also reduces the quality of lakes, rivers, and seas for boating, fishing, and swimming.

This soil loss reduces the capacity of farmland to grow crops. It also creates other costs. Irrigation systems, dams, and reservoirs clog up. **Silt** clogs waterways and harbors. Increased silt at the bottom of a harbor means smaller boats must be used to move cargo. Silt must eventually be removed to clear shipping channels for larger boats. All these factors increase the cost of shipping products. In the United States, the cost of damage from silt may exceed $10 billion a year.

Waste from mining pollutes land and water.

5 Fertilizer and Animal Runoff

The use of **inorganic** fertilizers has transformed agricultural production over the past 65 years. World fertilizer use increased from 14 million tons (12.7 million tonnes) in 1950 to 185.1 million tons (167.9 million tonnes) in 2008. Fertilizers fall into three main groups. They supply the three most basic mineral needs of plants, which are nitrogen, phosphorus, and potassium. Nitrogen in fertilizer comes in the form of nitrates.

Fertilizers can greatly increase crop **yields**. It is difficult to measure how much fertilizer plants actually need, however. Most farmers use more than is necessary. As a result, a large amount is wasted.

Some of the excess fertilizer runs through the soil and into the water supply. **Environmentalists** are especially concerned about nitrates. It has been estimated that one-fourth of all Europeans drink water with more nitrates in it than many scientists consider safe.

Fertilizer that flows into rivers, lakes, and coastal waters can also cause algae to grow. The algae suffocate aquatic plants and animals living there. They also block sunshine to other aquatic plants.

Farmers also apply a mix of animal feces, urine, and water, known as livestock slurry, to fields as fertilizer. They may also use sewage sludge from factories that treat wastewater. The sludge may contain harmful **heavy metals**, drugs, and other chemicals. In winter, the ground is frozen and too hard to absorb the nutrients in the livestock slurry and sewage sludge. Sometimes, slurry or sewage is washed into rivers or irrigation channels. People and other animals may get ill from drinking the water.

Nitrogen Fertilizer Use in the United States, 1964–2010

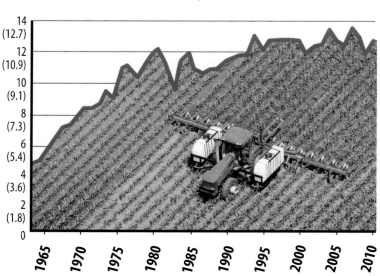

Should Farmers Be Allowed to Use Artificial Fertilizers and Pesticides?

Farmers have used chemicals for centuries. Since the 1940s, however, the industry that produces chemicals for farming has grown significantly. Natural soil rarely provides all that is required for large-scale agricultural production. It is usually necessary to add artificial supplements.

Pesticides have often reduced labor costs and improved yields. Traces of both artificial fertilizers and pesticides remain in the land for many years, however. They also show up in the food raised on this land. Scientists are concerned about the effect of these chemicals on health.

Industrial Farmers
We can use these chemicals safely. With the help of Global Positioning Systems and **Geographic Information Systems**, we can target plants with the precise amount of fertilizer that they need.

Physicians
It is important to grow large amounts of food, so people will have enough healthful food to eat. However, pesticides depend on the use of poisons. It is likely that some pesticides can harm humans, too.

Parents
We want food to be affordable, and large crops help keep prices lower. However, we also want to keep our children safe from the possible side effects of fertilizers and pesticides on our food. We cannot afford **organic food**.

Organic Farmers
We do not like the idea of putting chemicals on food crops. We feed the soil with organic matter instead of artificial fertilizers. We can produce foods with higher levels of vitamins and minerals.

For   Supportive   Undecided   Unsupportive   Against

What Soil Is Made Of

Soil is a complex material. It is made up of particles from rocks, minerals, water, and gases. It includes animal droppings and bits from dead plants and animals.

1 Rocks

The soil that covers Earth varies in quality and depth. In some areas, it is only 1 inch (2.5 centimeters) deep. In others, it may be as much as 66 feet (20 meters) deep. Only about one-third of the soil on Earth's surface can be used for agriculture. The rest is locked under the polar icecaps, is on mountains, or is in other remote places. These locations make it useless to farmers. Even the available soil varies greatly in value. Less than 10 percent is truly fertile. Most soil needs effort and careful management to produce crops.

The process of soil formation begins with the **weathering** of rock. Temperatures rise during the day and cool at night. Over time, these temperature changes cause large rocks to crack and break into smaller pieces. Water seeps into cracks in rocks, freezes, and expands, splitting rocks further. These actions produce a layer of loose material that is known as regolith.

The rock parts of soil are of three basic types. They are sand, silt, and clay. The amount of each of these types in an area affects the soil's fertility. Sand, silt, and clay are classified according to size. Sand can be further divided into coarse sand and fine sand. Particles more than 0.08 inches (2 millimeters) in diameter are classified as stones and are not part of true soil. Stones, however, often make up a high proportion of the material at or near the surface in a typical field.

Comparing Soil Particles

Look at the size of the different particles. If a particle of clay were the size of the dot, the silt and three kinds of sand would be the sizes shown. The proportions of these basic materials in a soil determine its texture. They also affect its ability to take up moisture, air, and nutrients.

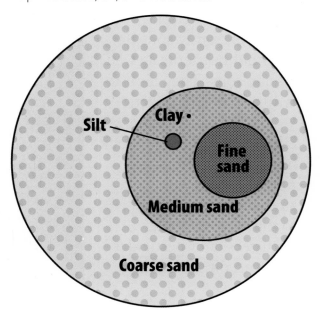

2 Minerals

More than two-thirds of Earth's rocks are made up of just three minerals. Feldspar accounts for about 51 percent, quartz for 12 percent, and mica for 5 percent. The weathering of quartz produces sand and silt. The weathering of mica and feldspar produces clay.

Clay soils tend to be rich in nutrients. Plowing and planting may be difficult in clay soils because they are so heavy. They also often crack. **Waterlogging** is a problem in clay soils, since they do not allow air to enter the soil.

Sandy soils are easy to cultivate, since they are light and water does not accumulate. Roots can easily penetrate sandy soil. However, sandy soils do not hold nutrients as well as clay soils. They tend to require more fertilizers.

Silty soils also tend to lack minerals and organic nutrients. They may clog, so that air cannot get to plant roots. Water, fertilizers, and pesticides may run off silty soils.

Loam is often regarded as the ideal agricultural soil. With a 20 percent clay content, it can hold moisture and nutrients. Made up of 40 percent sand, it also drains well and has pockets to hold air. The remaining 40 percent of loam is silt. The silt holds the clay and sand together. Loam provides an easily worked soil. It is fertile and resists erosion.

Loam is darker in color than sandy or silty soils.

3 Humus

Most plants depend on the soil for their nutrients. Natural soil nutrients come partly from minerals in rock particles and partly from **humus**. Moisture, air, and the action of tiny organisms in the clay and humus mixture allow plants to absorb these nutrients.

Life is sustained by soil and returns to it in a continuous process of recycling. As plants grow and mature, the leaves they shed add to the soil's richness. Decomposers, such as bacteria and fungi, break down the leaves into nutrients. Other plants can absorb these nutrients. Animals do their part as well. Their droppings add nutrients to the soil. When animals die, their bodies are broken down by decomposers, just as plant materials are.

Earthworms are critical to making good soil. They dig tunnels into the ground that aerate the dirt, bringing air into the soil. This action helps maintain the soil's fertility. Important decomposers, they eat plants and animals. In the **tropics**, termites perform a similar role.

Most soil organisms live in the top 8 inches (20 cm) of soil.

They can be killed or damaged by pesticides and even by fertilizers. Fertilizers, however, can help replace some of the fertility lost when the number of soil organisms is reduced.

The Living Soil

Healthy soil contains many different forms of life. Trillions of organisms might live in 35 cubic feet (1 cubic meter) of good soil, including the plants and animals listed below.

Microflora

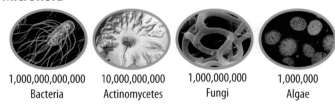

| 1,000,000,000,000 | 10,000,000,000 | 1,000,000,000 | 1,000,000 |
| Bacteria | Actinomycetes | Fungi | Algae |

Microfauna

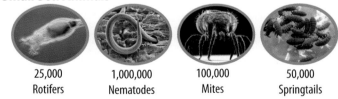

| 500,000,000,000 | 100,000,000,000 | 1,000,000 |
| Flagellates | Rhizopods | Ciliates |

Small Soil Animals

| 25,000 | 1,000,000 | 100,000 | 50,000 |
| Rotifers | Nematodes | Mites | Springtails |

Larger Soil Animals

| 50 | 50 | 50 |
| Slugs and snails | Spiders | Woodlice |

300	100	100	80
Centipedes	Beetles and their larvae	Fly larvae	Earthworms
	150 Other Insects		

4 Pesticides and Fertilizers

Farmers have used fertilizers to enrich the soil and improve plant growth for hundreds of years. Before the mid-1700s, all farming was organic. It relied on recycling plant and animal materials. Farmers plowed dead plants and animal manure into the soil. This process added nutrients. It also disposed of unwanted waste. Sometimes, other fertilizers were used. However, they were made from such natural substances as potash, which is a form of potassium, and bird or bat droppings. The discovery that nitrates and **urea** could be used as fertilizers transformed agriculture. It meant that crop production could be increased with the use of these chemicals.

Pesticides destroy or control many types of pests, including mice, insects, fungi, weeds, and bacteria. Pesticides have substantially increased farming productivity.

For example, today, tending 2.5 acres (1 hectare) of corn takes only one-sixth the labor required before chemical weed killers were developed. Herbicides, or weed killers, account for almost half of all pesticides sold. **Insecticides** account for a further 25 to 30 percent. Poisons that kill fungi and other special chemicals make up the rest of the market. Pesticides have also reduced populations of birds, earthworms, bees, and other organisms. The chemicals in pesticides can kill or injure these animals.

As with fertilizers, farmers tend to use more pesticide than is necessary. Fruits and vegetables are often sprayed to make sure that they look good. Skin flaws on these products greatly reduce the selling price, even though the blemishes do not mean the food cannot be eaten. "Insurance" spraying is widely practiced on other crops as well, to reduce any risk that pests will harm the crops.

Some insecticides are poisons that act on the nervous systems of bees.

Should Use of Some Pesticides Be Stopped to Protect Species?

Over the millions of years that life has existed on Earth, animal species have often become extinct. Scientists believe, however, that the rate of extinction is much higher today than at most times in the past. Some scientists have estimated that human actions have sped up this rate by about 1,000 times.

Pesticides target specific insects and other animals that destroy crops. However, they have been shown to harm other species as well. Frogs and other amphibians often die off in reaction to these chemicals. Many types of birds, bats, bees, and other animals are also affected.

Environmentalists
With the extinction of species, we are losing possible valuable resources. Removing any species from an ecosystem can be destructive. If an ecosystem's delicate balance is upset, rainfall and air and soil quality can be affected.

Citizens
We need our woodlands, fields, and clean water for recreation and for future **generations**. Runoff that contains harmful chemicals from pesticides put those resources in danger. Governments should enforce rules to keep land abuse at a minimum.

Farmers
We need fertilizers and pesticides to improve our crop yields, but they have unplanned side effects. Insects that pollinate our crops are dying. We need research on new fertilizers and pesticides to reduce the negative effects of current products.

Agricultural Business Leaders
We must do our best to save the species that we can. However, it is most important to produce the largest amount of food we can in order to feed the billions of people on the planet. Human life is more important than specific species.

| For | Supportive | Undecided | Unsupportive | Against |

5 Toxic Additions

Fertilizers and pesticides have value if used correctly. Other additions to the soil have only a negative impact. Most pollution eventually finds its way into the soil. The waste created by modern society is routinely buried in the ground. In the United States, people generate about 250 million tons (227 million tonnes) of municipal solid waste a year. More than 85 million tons (77 million tonnes) of this material is recycled and **composted**. Most of the rest is buried in landfill sites each year. As the material in landfills decomposes, it may leave toxic chemicals in the soil. Many landfill sites are not properly sealed.

Factory farms are huge operations. Billions of cows, chickens, and pigs are raised in industrial settings. Many of these animals are kept in small pens. Some factory farms process millions of animals each year. Feedlots are one form of factory farm. Young cattle are brought in and fed grains that promote quick growth. Antibiotics and **growth hormones** are added to their feed. Sometimes, heavy metals such as mercury and cadmium are also present in the feed.

Livestock and poultry factory farms produce an estimated 500 million tons (454 tonnes) of manure each year. Unlike human sewage, this manure is untreated. Most manure from these factory farms is spread on agricultural land, which cannot absorb this much material. Chemicals, such as antibiotics, hormones, and other additions to animal feed, seep into the ground.

People then eat both the animals raised on factory farms and the crops from land spread with their manure. If consumed in large amounts, mercury and cadmium can cause health problems for people. Excess antibiotics can lead to the development of **superbugs**.

> "Billions of cows, chickens, and pigs are raised in industrial settings."

The typical farm produced five types of animals for sale in the early 1900s. Now, it produces one.

Is Factory Farming an Acceptable Way to Treat Animals and the Land?

Around the globe, factory farms raise more than 50 percent of the world's pork and poultry. Feedlots produce 43 percent of the world's beef. In the United States, these operations are also called concentrated animal feeding operations (CAFOs). A single, large CAFO can hold more than 55,000 turkeys or 1,000 cattle. CAFOs produce large amounts of food and also large amounts of waste.

Feedlot Owners

Diets around the world have changed. Meat has become an everyday item, not an occasional treat. It also contains important nutrients, such as protein. Factory farms are the only way to produce meat cheaply enough for many consumers to afford it. They also provide jobs for thousands of people.

Governments

People need affordable sources of protein, and factory farming provides inexpensive meat and poultry. We can also supervise large operations more cheaply than small-scale farms that raise animals. We try to make sure the animals suffer as little as possible and that animal waste is disposed of safely.

Consumers

We need to have affordable meat. Factory farms may produce cheap meat, but they also create a great deal of waste. This waste may harm the land and our health. Hormones in feedlot-produced meat may be causing some illnesses. We are also concerned about the discomfort the animals feel.

Animal Rights Activists

It is wrong to treat animals the way factory farms do. Chickens have their beaks cut off to keep the birds from harming each other. Pigs' tails are removed to prevent infection from bites by other pigs. In addition, the damage to the land from animal waste will take many years to correct.

| For | Supportive | Undecided | Unsupportive | Against |

Land Use and Abuse

KEY CONCEPTS

1 Intensive Farming

2 Heavy Machinery

3 Slash-and-Burn Farming

4 Wind and Rainfall

5 Pesticides

Farming and other forms of land use can create many problems, including erosion and damage to soil. Rainfall and wind carry away billions of tons of Earth's topsoil every year. Heavy rainfall washes soil into rivers that may move it thousands of miles to the sea. Industrial and urban waste poisons the land. Plants are cut down in dry areas, and their roots can no longer hold the soil in place.

1 Intensive Farming

In the past, many farmers followed the practice known as mixed farming. They planted a variety of crops in their fields. They often changed the crop grown in a certain field from year to year because different crops take different nutrients out of the soil. Some years they allowed a field to go **fallow** and grazed animals on it. Mixed farming helps conserve the nutrients in the soil and allows nutrients that have been used up to be naturally restored.

Many traditional mixed farms have been replaced by large farms growing one crop or businesses raising one kind of animal. These intensive farming methods allow a small number of people to produce vast quantities of food. By reducing the number of crops or types of animals being raised, businesses can usually raise more of one species. This allows them to make more money than traditional mixed farms can.

Growing one crop year after year on the same land requires adding large amounts of fertilizers to the soil. All these additions to the farmland filter down into the soil. From there, they are taken up by plants and other animals, which humans eat. Some of the chemicals enter underground water supplies that people use for drinking and cooking. People also breathe in some of the farming chemicals.

Intensive farming often requires irrigation, which can wash dirt away and reduce soil nutrients.

By focusing on raising one profitable crop on hundreds of acres (ha), industrial farming corporations can afford many huge machines.

2 Heavy Machinery

Large farms require the use of big farming machines. To allow the machines easy access, fields are enlarged. Hedgerows are tightly growing wild bushes and trees that surround fields. These are cut down. Instead of small areas of land anchored by the surrounding plants, there are giant open fields. In times of very dry weather, winds blow across these open expanses and lift off the topsoil.

Hedgerows are important for many kinds of wildlife. In Great Britain, for example, hedgerows may support about 80 percent of the woodland birds, 50 percent of the mammals, and 30 percent of the butterflies found in the country. In many nations, these strips of land are decreasing in size and number yearly. With the loss of hedgerows comes a loss of wildlife.

The use of tractors and other forms of heavy machinery has also packed down the soil over large areas. This reduces the soil's ability to absorb moisture and air. It is difficult for plant roots to penetrate compacted soil. Their ability to absorb nutrients is reduced. Deep plowing also leaves loose material on the surface where it can easily be eroded.

Should Landowners Be Allowed to Use Any Farming Practice They Want?

In **developed countries**, large farms owned by huge companies have become commonplace. In the United States, the number of farms has fallen by 63 percent since the early 1900s. During that same time, the average farm size has increased by 67 percent.

In **developing countries**, small family farms are more common. They grow several crops to feed the family and to sell at local markets. However, the number of large farms run by businesses is increasing rapidly in these countries.

Industrial Farming Corporations

Our goal is to make the highest profit for our investors, so the land must produce as much as it can. We are also making more food at a lower cost. We should be able to use our land the way we think is best.

Family Farmers

Our land was passed down to us from our grandparents. To make enough money, we need to use artificial fertilizers. We use these chemicals as wisely as possible. We also want to make sure our grandchildren can farm the land.

Environmentalists

Awareness of environmental issues should include much greater concern for soil quality. The costs of soil contamination should be taken into account when considering what farm owners should be able to do on their land.

American Indian Groups

People who use land today must think about the effects their actions will have on future generations. Will our children's children be able to safely live off the land? Anything that damages the land now is a problem for them.

| For | Supportive | Undecided | Unsupportive | Against |

3 Slash-and-Burn Farming

Slash-and-burn agriculture is a method of clearing land for farming. Trees and other plants are cut down and burned. About 250 million people around the world use slash-and-burn farming.

Farmers in the tropics have often used slash-and-burn techniques to clear parts of tropical rainforests. These actions can quickly produce areas of desert. The soil in tropical rainforests is usually thin and of poor quality. The small amounts of nutrients in it are used up quickly. After two or three years, the farmer leaves the first plot, moves to a new area, and cuts down and burns more trees.

In the Amazon Rainforest of Brazil and other South American countries, slash-and-burn techniques are also used to clear land for raising cattle. Grass is planted for the cattle to eat. Scientists estimate that ranchers must clear about 55 square feet (5 square meters) of rainforest to produce the meat needed to make a ¼-pound (113-gram) hamburger. However, the soil is not fertile enough to support grass for more than a few years. Without the trees to hold down the soil, it gradually erodes from wind and rainfall.

Small clearings can be reclaimed by new growth, though this may take 40 to 45 years. In larger open areas, however, the soil becomes so depleted that plants cannot survive. The thin soil is soon washed away, leaving a desert-like area. In many hilly regions of the developing world, deforestation on steep slopes has also resulted in landslides. Soil falls into rivers and is swept downstream.

Burning trees and plants adds some nutrients to the soil, but they are used up quickly. Poor farmers cannot afford fertilizers to replace these nutrients.

Should Worldwide Organizations Help Control Land Erosion?

Nongovernmental organizations, or NGOs, are national and international groups that focus on specific issues. They may concentrate on reducing world hunger, protecting species, educating girls and women, and many other issues. Some, such as the International Erosion Control Association, focus on educating people and nations about the issues of erosion.

The traditional practice of leaving fields fallow in certain years is now relatively rare. Many farmers are under great financial pressure. They cannot afford the kind of long-term care of the land that was once more common.

NGOs
Land-abuse issues cross national borders. We can suggest policies that help governments deal with erosion control. We can also fund farming and erosion-control programs using these policies.

Environmentalists
NGOs can take several countries' solutions to land-abuse problems and use them in other countries. Their data and policy suggestions can help governments make good decisions about safely growing more food.

Governments
We are protecting our people and our land. NGOs have good intentions, but we will not give control of our land to organizations that are not based here. They do not know our problems as well as we do.

Local Farmers
Some of our families have lived on this land for centuries. We can take care of it ourselves. We know more about what practices work locally. People from organizations outside of our country do not know our soil.

| For | Supportive | Undecided | Unsupportive | Against |

4 Wind and Rainfall

Every year, more than 22 billion tons (20 billion tonnes) of soil are swept away by wind and precipitation. Storms take up soil loosened by poor farming and herding techniques. They can carry that dirt for hundreds or even thousands of miles. For example, eroded soil that blows off African farms, dry lands, and deserts now settles on South America.

When too many herds of cows, sheep, and goats graze on grasslands, desertification can result. Two areas in particular are rapidly becoming deserts. One lies in southern China and northern Mongolia, and the other is the Sahel in Africa. China's goat herds have expanded rapidly since the mid-1980s. Goats can survive on sparse plant life. They eat plants down to the soil level. As a result, the plants' root systems often die, and plant roots no longer hold the dirt in place. Spring winds carry the soil across China to Korea, Japan, and even North America. In 2006, a windstorm dumped 330,000 tons (299,000 tonnes) of dust on the Chinese capital of Beijing.

Intensive farming and herding on already dry lands is damaging much of Africa. Nigeria alone loses 868,000 acres (351,300 ha) to desertification each year.

Acid rain is precipitation that is polluted by acid in the atmosphere. The three most common chemicals that cause acid rain are sulfur, carbon, and nitrogen. When these chemicals combine with moisture in the air, they form sulfuric acid, carbonic acid, and nitric acid. They are produced when oil, coal, and natural gas are burned.

These acids damage the environment, affecting soil fertility. The acids in the rain dissolve nutrients and minerals in the soil that plants need. The rain then washes those nutrients and minerals out of the soil. Acid rain also harms plants, animals, and the surfaces of buildings.

Once acid rain weakens a tree, it is more likely to die from drought, insects burrowing into it, or germs that cause illnesses.

5 Pesticides

Weed control has always presented a big challenge to farmers. In the past, farmers regularly hoed their crops by hand. This chore took a great deal of time. The only available weed killers, or herbicides, were sea salt, by-products of chemical industries, and various oils. By the middle of the 20th century, scientists had developed more effective herbicides.

Yet the widespread and careless use of such chemicals damaged both farmlands and human health. Overuse can create problems. Over time, many pests are able to resist the chemicals. The pesticides become less effective.

The chemical glyphosate, also known as Roundup, has been a boon to farmers. It kills many kinds of weeds and is easy to use. However, some weeds, such as pigweed, are beginning to be resistant to glyphosate. Pigweed can grow up to 3 inches (7.6 cm) a day. Many pigweed plants grow to 7 feet (2.1 m). They can cover crops and reduce their access to sunlight and water.

Pesticides are often sprayed through the air or applied directly on fields. The chemicals may float through the air and be inhaled. Most pesticides are toxic and are often dangerous to humans, animals, and the environment. Modern pesticides are designed to break down quickly after contact with the soil. Some pesticides, however, can remain in the environment for 20 years or more.

Workers must wear special clothing and gear to protect them from the harmful effects of some pesticides sprayed on crops.

Mapping Land Use and Abuse

Pacific Ocean

North America

Atlantic Ocean

Increasing Demand, Decreasing Ability to Produce

According to the United Nations, worldwide demand for agricultural products will grow by 70 percent in the first half of the 21st century. However, over the centuries, 7.8 million square miles (20.2 million sq. km) of soil have been degraded through human activities. Without changes in agriculture and efforts to protect the soil, the land may not be able to supply all the food that will be needed.

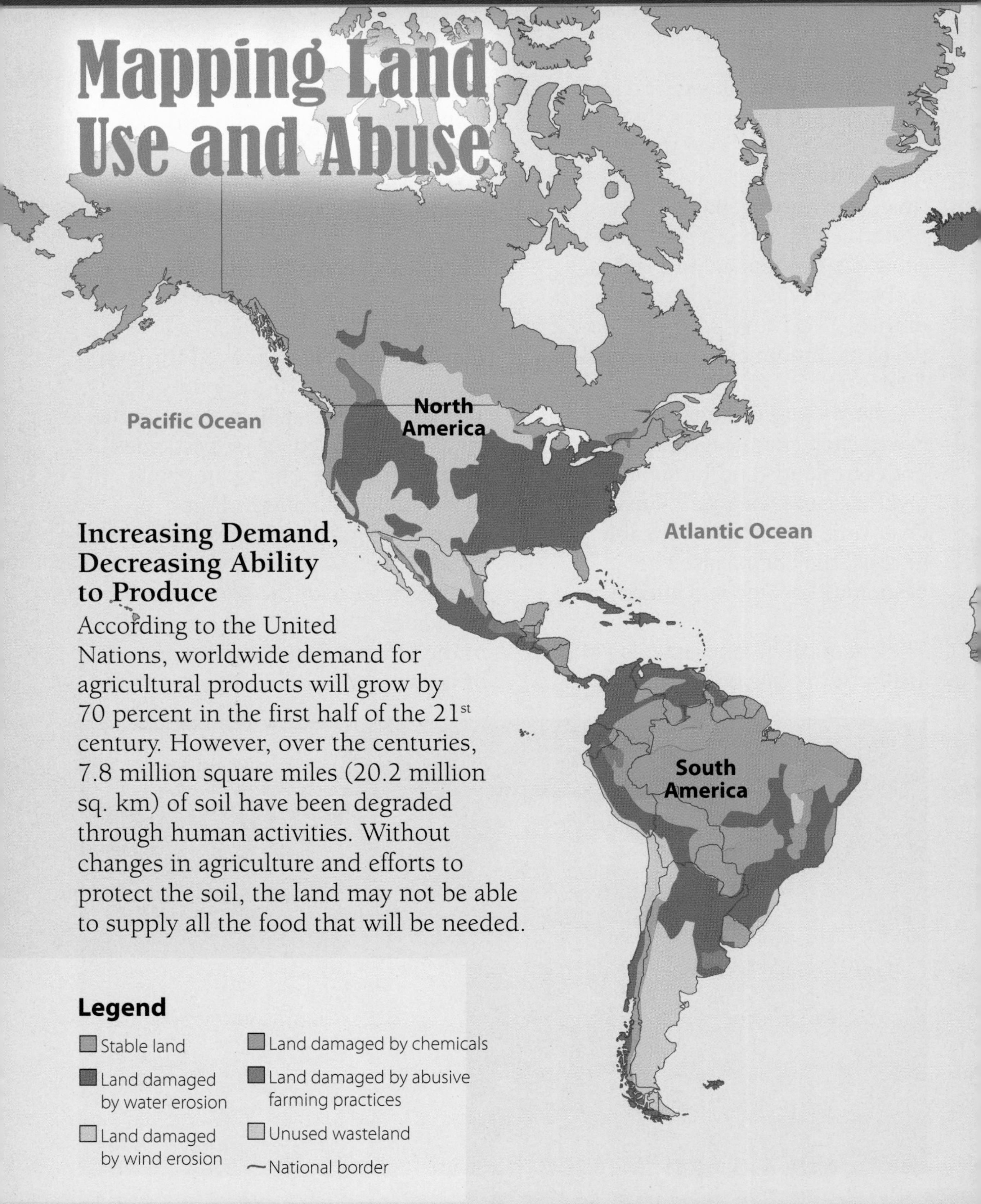

South America

Legend

- Stable land
- Land damaged by water erosion
- Land damaged by wind erosion
- Land damaged by chemicals
- Land damaged by abusive farming practices
- Unused wasteland
- National border

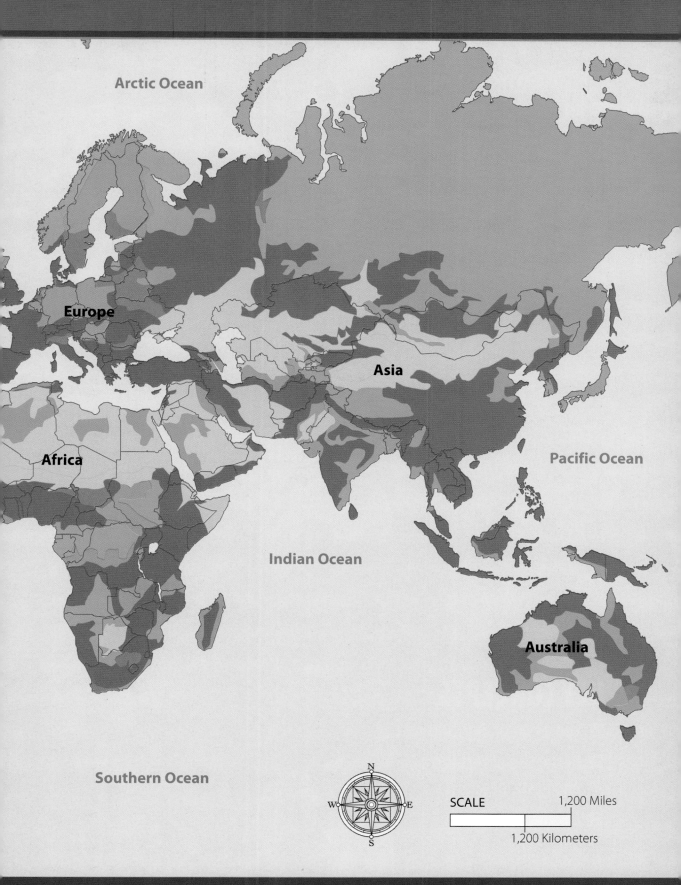

Arctic Ocean

Europe

Asia

Africa

Pacific Ocean

Indian Ocean

Australia

Southern Ocean

SCALE

1,200 Miles

1,200 Kilometers

Protecting the Soil

KEY CONCEPTS

1 Conservation Agriculture

2 Better Use of Fertilizers and Pesticides

3 Less Reliance on Single Crops

In addition to reducing nutrients in soil, intensive farming also causes pollution. Yet the demand for increasing quantities of affordable food makes it impossible for agriculture to return to small, mixed farms. Science has not been able to provide a quick solution to these problems. What steps can be taken to reduce agricultural practices that harm the land?

1 Conservation Agriculture

Simple techniques, such as reducing plowing, hedging fields with grass, and planting trees, can cut erosion by 50 percent. Covering entire fields with mulch provided by the stalks, stems, and other waste matter from harvested crops can also help reduce erosion. Mulching keeps the ground moist and adds nutrients to the soil.

Some farmers alternate the types of crops they grow in a certain area every year. This technique, called crop rotation, has been used for thousands of years. To benefit from rotation, the plants chosen should not use the same soil nutrients. Rotation also helps to keep crops healthy, since pests that feed on one type of plant may not be able to survive on another. With crop rotation, there is less need to let fields lie fallow or to apply artificial fertilizers.

Many governments around the world are encouraging the use of conservation agriculture (CA). Farms using CA do little or no tilling. Seeds are drilled directly into the soil with zero tillage planters. Surface mulch keeps in water and heat. The soil is protected from erosion and can regain its natural balance and fertility. CA uses pesticides and fertilizers where necessary. Once CA is established, the need to add chemicals can be greatly reduced.

Leading Countries Using Conservation Agriculture

More than 451,700 square miles (1.17 million sq. km) of land across the world are currently farmed using CA methods. These techniques are most widely used in North America, South America, and Australia.

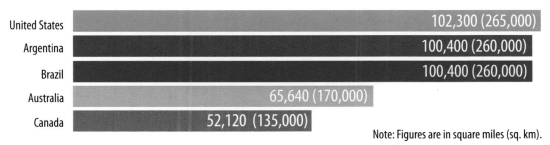

	Square miles (sq. km)
United States	102,300 (265,000)
Argentina	100,400 (260,000)
Brazil	100,400 (260,000)
Australia	65,640 (170,000)
Canada	52,120 (135,000)

Note: Figures are in square miles (sq. km).

2 Better Use of Fertilizers and Pesticides

Nature adapts. Insects and weeds become resistant to pesticides. Control efforts can never succeed completely. New pests and diseases appear as the old ones are defeated.

Integrated pest management (IPM) uses a variety of methods to control pests. Farmers may release insects or other organisms that prey on specific pests. They may use **sterile** males to control insect populations. In one program, the introduction of natural predators reduced cassava mealybug infestations in Africa. The benefits of the program hugely outweighed the costs of the predators. Different farming methods can reduce the number of pests. Another approach that is being used is **bioengineering**. Scientists are developing crops that can fend off specific pests and weeds.

3 Less Reliance on Single Crops

Single-crop farming breaks down the ecological balance that diversity of plant life usually provides. Such diversity can be achieved in farming by mosaic cropping.

In mosaic cropping, rows of one plant are grown in between rows of another plant.

With plants of different heights and sizes, it is harder to move machinery through land planted with mosaic cropping. However, the system is closer to the way plants grow naturally. One important advantage is that the pest problem tends to be reduced by natural competition. When several plants are grown in one area, a variety of organisms can live in between plants and in the soil. Different predators can reduce prey that harms crops.

Mixing carrot and onion plants reduces carrot flies, aphids, and other insects that damage these crops.

Can Bioengineering Improve Industrial Farming Safely?

Bioengineering uses technology to alter **genes** in organisms. These organisms may include plants, animals, and bacteria. Bioengineering combines desirable genes from one species with the genes of another species.

For example, irrigation slowly raises the salt level, or salinity, in fields. Using bioengineering, scientists have recently developed a type of tomato plant that can grow in salty soil. The soil's salt content can be as much as 50 times higher than the level tomatoes normally tolerate.

Bioengineering Companies

We can design crops that look and taste better. They will be able to resist diseases and pests. We can produce animals that yield more meat, eggs, and milk. They will need fewer growth hormones and antibiotics.

Industrial Farmers

Bioengineered crops and animals will increase our ability to grow more food. They will help us rely less on pesticides, fertilizers, growth hormones, and antibiotics. However, the current costs of bioengineered seeds and chemicals are high.

Consumers

We do not yet know what health effects these bioengineered crops and animals may have on us. They may increase our food allergies. Some health effects of eating bioengineered foods may not become known for years.

Environmentalists

The long-term effects of new varieties of plants and animals in our environment cannot be known. Bioengineered organisms may have a harmful impact on their ecosystems that scientists cannot predict.

| For | Supportive | Undecided | Unsupportive | Against |

Land Use and Soil Erosion through History

For most of recorded history, people have used the land the way they wished. They cut down forests and farmed the land or grazed animals. If the land became unusable, they just moved on to a new, untouched area. Over the past several hundred years, this way of life has become impossible. As the population has increased, greater quantities of food must be produced. If erosion and land abuse make some land unusable, there are fewer and fewer new places to go.

500 BC

1931
Severe drought hits the Midwest and the southern plains of the United States. As crops die, dust from the overplowed and overgrazed land begins to blow, creating a "dust bowl."

500 BC
Greek coastal cities become cut off from the sea after deforestation causes soil erosion. Silt fills in bays and the mouths of rivers.

1928
Soil erosion is identified as a serious threat to agricultural productivity in the United States. The U.S. Congress provides funds to the USDA for soil erosion research.

1934
The United States experiences its worst drought in history. Dust storms destroy about 35 million acres (14 million ha) of cultivated land.

AD 1862
The United States Department of Agriculture (USDA) is created. It works to protect farmers' income and soil and water resources.

1931

2002

1935

The U.S. Congress declares soil erosion "a national menace." The Soil Conservation Service is established. Today, this agency is called the Natural Resources Conservation Service.

1945

The United Nations forms the Food and Agriculture Organization to help nations improve their agricultural practices.

1945–1990

A study by the United Nations estimates that 38 percent of the world's cropland is degraded, including 74 percent in Central America.

1970

The U.S. Environmental Protection Agency is established to protect human health and to safeguard the natural environment.

2002

It is estimated that forest cover in the developing world had fallen by 800,000 square miles (2 million sq. km) since 1980.

2002

The European Forum on Agricultural Research for Development reports that two-thirds of agricultural land has been affected by soil degradation over the past 50 years.

2004

Members of the Stockholm Convention on Persistent Organic Pollutants seek to end use of a number of dangerous pesticides.

2011

The world population passes 7 billion, according to an estimate by the U.S. Census Bureau.

2012

The largest United Nations conference in history, the UN Conference on **Sustainable** Development, is held in Rio de Janeiro, Brazil. It promotes a stronger role in policy-making for women, NGOs, and small-scale food farmers.

2012

Working on Erosion and Land Use

SOIL SCIENTIST

Duties To promote soil health and conservation

Education A bachelor's or master's degree in agricultural science, soil science, or a related field

Interest Protecting land and the environment

Soil scientists study the relationship of soil to the climate and the environment. They collect soil in the field and analyze samples. Soil scientists see if the soil will support agriculture, ecosystems, and buildings. They also check for pollutants. These scientists recommend actions based on this information.

Soil scientists work in different areas. Some study bacteria in the soil and their effect on soil fertility. Some soil scientists work with government agencies to decide how land should be used. Others work to prevent soil loss.

AGRICULTURAL ENGINEER

Duties To improve farming equipment and agricultural products while conserving soil and water

Education A bachelor's or master's degree in biological or agricultural science engineering

Interest Using design to protect the environment and increase crop production

Agricultural engineers solve farming problems, such as erosion. They use biology, engineering principles, and design skills. Agricultural engineers need solid scientific knowledge and math skills. They must also be creative to develop solutions to environmental problems.

Agricultural engineers work with farmers and the farming industry. They recommend the most efficient methods of farming to conserve soil and water and to reduce pollution. Some agricultural engineers design new types of equipment to reduce harm to the soil.

ENVIRONMENT ECONOMIST

Duties Studies trends in how natural resources, such as water and soil, are used; recommends to policy-makers the best ways to use and protect these resources

Education A bachelor's or master's degree in economics and environmental studies

Interest Math, data analysis, environmental protection

Most environmental issues also concern money and the economy. Environmental economists analyze the value of natural resources. They compare both their financial value and their environmental value. These results help governments and organizations decide if environmental policies are sound. They help answer questions, such as whether or not these policies will benefit jobs, public health, and the environment.

Environmental economists use their research skills to examine statistics. They use computers to make models of what may happen. These economists must have good communication skills.

AGRICULTURAL BIOENGINEER

Duties Create new varieties of plants and animals that produce more food

Education A bachelor's, master's, or doctorate in bioengineering or biology and engineering

Interest Biology, genetics, solving problems related to raising enough food and improving soil, water, and air

Agricultural bioengineers develop new types of plants, animals, and other organisms. They must consider the impact of their work on soil, water, and air quality. They work with genes from plants and animals to solve problems with food production. Skills include research and the ability to analyze large amounts of data. Bioengineers must be willing to experiment with different techniques. Most agricultural bioengineers work in labs as well as out in the field.

Key Soil Protection Agencies

FAO

Goal Improving agricultural productivity

Reach Worldwide

Facts More than 180 member countries

The **Food and Agriculture Organization (FAO)** of the United Nations works to increase investments in agriculture. It helps countries plan, apply, and increase sustainable agriculture. One of its main goals is to be a center for information. The staff includes scientists who study soil management and farming. Some of its workers specialize in managing fish populations, forests, and livestock. The FAO staff also includes nutritionists, social scientists, economists, statisticians, and other professionals. These people collect, analyze, and present data. This information helps member countries plan their farming and soil protection policies.

ISRIC

Goal Provide information about the world's soil resources

Reach Worldwide

Facts Developing historical and modern-day maps of soil types to track erosion and other issues

The **International Soil Reference and Information Centre (ISRIC)** is an independent organization that was founded in 1964. The original organizers were the International Soil Science Society and the United Nations Educational, Scientific, and Cultural Organization (UNESCO). ISRIC World Soil Information provides information about the planet's soil resources. It focuses on soil data and mapping. ISRIC also trains and educates researchers, managers, and users of soil data. It focuses on conserving soil and preventing erosion worldwide.

IECA

Goal To help countries solve problems caused by erosion and sediment

Reach Worldwide

Facts A resource for people who want to prevent and control erosion.

The **International Erosion Control Association (IECA)** is the world's oldest and largest organization concerned with erosion and sediment that results from erosion. Its SOIL Fund program gives money for a number of purposes. It funds research into the impact of erosion and ways to control it. It provides money to educate those who seek to stop erosion and to develop new techniques. It also funds projects to help communities who have been affected by erosion and sediment.

UNEP

Goal To help people and nations care for the environment today and for the future

Reach Worldwide

Facts Works in the Congo River basin in Africa, the world's second-largest rainforest, to reduce deforestation and habitat loss

The **United Nations Environment Programme (UNEP)** considers ecosystems as a whole, including their value to humans. It encourages farmers, developers, and governments to look at more than just the money-making ability of land. UNEP urges them to work together in ways that will improve both the land and people's lives. Sustainability is at the heart of UNEP's mission. It also works to keep toxic chemicals out of the soil and reduce deforestation.

Rajendra PACHA

Research a Soil Conservation Issue

The Issue

Land use and soil erosion is a subject of much debate. Many groups may not agree on the best way to protect the land. It is important to enter into a discussion to hear all the points of view before making decisions. Discussing issues will ensure that the actions taken are beneficial for all involved.

Get the Facts

Choose an issue (Political, Ethical, Cultural, or Ecological) from this book. Then, pick one of the four groups presented in the issue spectrum. Using the book and research in the library or the Internet, find out more about its point of view. What is important to the group? Why is it backing or opposing the particular issue? What claims or facts can it use to support its point of view? Be sure to write clear and concise supporting arguments for your group. Focus on the environment and how the group's needs relate to it. Will this group be affected in a positive or negative way by changes in the environment around it?

Use the Concept Web

A concept web is a useful research tool. Read the information and review the structure in the concept web on the next page. Use the relationships between concepts to help you understand your group's point of view.

Organize Your Research

Sort your information into organized points. Make sure your research clearly answers what impact the issue will have on your chosen group, how that impact will affect it, and why the group has chosen its specific point of view.

SOIL CONSERVATION CONCEPT WEB

Use this concept web to understand the network of factors contributing to land use and soil erosion issues.

- Low- or no-tillage methods
- Crop rotation improves soil
- Fertilizer and pesticide use reduced or eliminated
- Mosaic cropping is more like nature

- Mulching
- Natural fertilizers and pest control
- Bioengineering
- Reduce runoff

- Municipal and industrial wastes
- Pesticides and inorganic fertilizers from intensive farming
- Factory-farm runoff

Sustainable Agriculture

Soil Contamination

Soil Protection

Soil Nature

Land Use and Soil Erosion

Soil Erosion

- Weathering of rocks
- Minerals
- Humus created from decaying plants and animals

Soil Life

- Desertification and deforestation
- Population growth that uses the land
- Plant cover removed, exposing soil
- Water and wind remove soil
- Intensive farming harms nutrients in soil

- Sustains life
- Recycling of dead plant and animal life enriches soil
- Pollution disturbs health of humans, other animals, and plants

Intensive Agriculture

- Factory farming and single crops
- Compacting of soil makes it hard for roots to penetrate dirt
- Deep plowing disturbs ecosystems

Test Your Knowledge

Answer each of the questions below to test your knowledge of land use and soil erosion.

1 Why is soil important to life on Earth?

2 What are three natural components of soil?

3 How much of Earth's land is fertile enough to farm?

4 What do worms do for the soil?

5 What are growth hormones?

6 What is crop rotation?

7 What are the three minerals that plants need most?

8 What is the best soil for growing crops?

9 What do pesticides do?

10 What is slash-and-burn agriculture?

ANSWERS 1. It supports plant and animal life. **2.** Rocks, minerals, and humus. **3.** 10 percent. **4.** They aerate the soil and help keep it fertile. **5.** Chemicals that make animals grow faster **6.** Changing crops every growing season. **7.** Nitrogen, phosphorus, and potassium **8.** Loam **9.** They kill pests that attack crops, including mice, insects, fungi, weeds, and bacteria. **10.** Cutting down trees and other plants and burning them to create agricultural land

5

10

8

4

1

Key Words

aquatic: growing in or living near water

bioengineering: changing the traits of an organism by adding to or subtracting from its genes.

composted: put decayed plant matter on fields to fertilize land

contaminated: made something impure or unfit for use by adding something harmful

degradation: a lessening of usefulness or power

developed countries: countries with high average income and advanced technology

developing countries: countries with low average income that until recently had little manufacturing and technology

environmentalists: people who are interested in protecting the environment

fallow: cropland allowed to lie without sowing for one or more seasons

fungi: living things, such as molds and mushrooms, that live on dead or decaying plants and animals

generations: groups of living beings that make up a step in a line from one ancestor

genes: tiny units of a cell that determine the characteristics of an organism

Geographic Information Systems: computer systems that work with geographic information and that allow users to analyze and edit data

growth hormones: chemicals in plants or animals that controls how fast they grow

heavy metals: chemicals that build up in the food chain and can have toxic effects on organisms

humus: part of the soil made from partially decayed plant or animal matter

inorganic: made up of matter that does not come from dead or living plants or animals

insecticides: chemicals used to kill insects

minerals: chemical elements that occur in nature and are not related to plants or animals. Minerals are usually found in the ground.

nitrates: chemical compounds made up of nitrogen and oxygen

nutrients: things needed by people, plants, and animals to live and grow

organic food: food produced without the use of artificial fertilizers or pesticides

pesticides: chemicals used to destroy insects and other organisms that harm crops or animals

phytoplankton: tiny plant life in water

precipitation: water that falls to the earth in the form of rain, snow, sleet, or hail

silt: tiny particles of sand, clay, or other materials in water

sterile: unable to make young

superbugs: germs that can resist antibiotics

sustainable: a method of harvesting or using a resource so that it does not run out or become damaged forever

tilling: preparing and cultivating soil, for example by plowing

topsoil: the fertile upper layer of soil

tropics: a warm region of Earth that is near the equator

urea: a substance that contains nitrogen and dissolves in water

waterlogging: soaking of agricultural land caused by too much water in the soil

weathering: wearing away or changing the appearance of something by exposing it to wind, rain, and cold

yields: the amount of particular crops produced in specific areas of land

Index

Log on to www.av2books.com

AV² by Weigl brings you media enhanced books that support active learning. Go to www.av2books.com, and enter the special code found on page 2 of this book. You will gain access to enriched and enhanced content that supplements and complements this book. Content includes video, audio, weblinks, quizzes, a slide show, and activities.

AV² Online Navigation

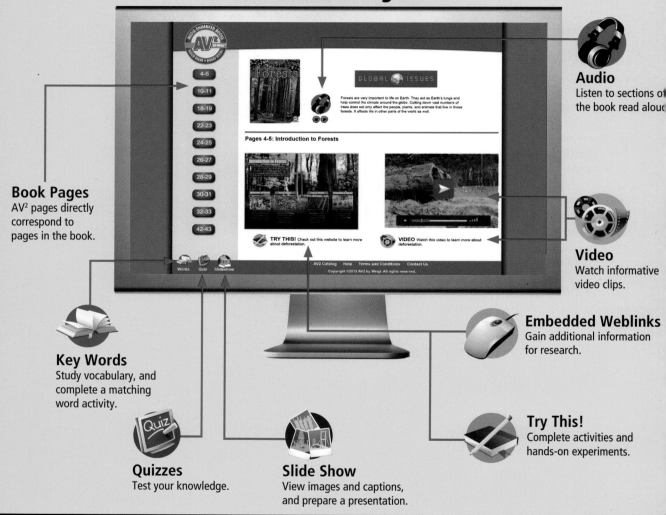

Book Pages
AV² pages directly correspond to pages in the book.

Audio
Listen to sections of the book read aloud.

Video
Watch informative video clips.

Key Words
Study vocabulary, and complete a matching word activity.

Embedded Weblinks
Gain additional information for research.

Quizzes
Test your knowledge.

Slide Show
View images and captions, and prepare a presentation.

Try This!
Complete activities and hands-on experiments.

AV² was built to bridge the gap between print and digital. We encourage you to tell us what you like and what you want to see in the future.

Sign up to be an AV² Ambassador at www.av2books.com/ambassador.